LOST TRAMWAYS OF ENGLAND
BRIGHTON

PETER WALLER

GRAFFEG

CONTENTS

BRIGHTON

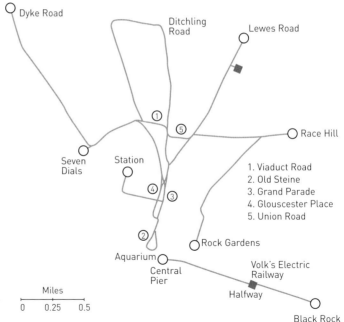

1. Viaduct Road
2. Old Steine
3. Grand Parade
4. Glouscester Place
5. Union Road

Miles
0   0.25   0.5

INTRODUCTION

Although there had been street tramways in Britain from the early 1860s in places like Birkenhead and London, it was not until the 1870 Tramways Act that a legislative framework was established for their construction and operation. The Act empowered local authorities to grant licences to companies to operate tramways for a 21-year period. The licensee could construct the tramway itself or the route could be constructed by the local authority and leased as part of the franchise to the operator. Initially, it was expected that private companies would always operate the tramways built; however, in 1883, Huddersfield Corporation in the West Riding of Yorkshire, having constructed a new steam tramway to serve the town, was unable to find a licensee willing to take on operation and so became the first municipal operator of trams within the British Isles.

The 1870 Act imposed a number of restrictions upon the tramway builder and operator; with the benefit of hindsight, it can be seen that these had a negative impact upon tramway development in the United Kingdom and undoubtedly represented one factor in the demise of the tramcar from the 1920s onwards. One of these clauses required the builder and operator of the tramway to maintain the public highway to a distance of 18 inches outside each running line; this effectively made the tramway owner responsible for the upkeep of the road surface on those streets where trams operated. At a time when the condition of the public highway was often poor, the well-built and well-maintained section over which the trams operated became a magnet for other road users. As road traffic increased, so trams – despite the fact that the road had been constructed to accommodate them – were increasingly perceived as a cause of road traffic delays.

The second weakness within the 1870 Act was the so-called 'scrap iron clause'; this permitted the licensor – usually the local authority – to take over the assets (such as the trams) owned by the licensee at asset value – including depreciation – rather than reflecting the value of the business. As a result, tramway licensees became increasingly unwilling to invest in their business as the licence period came towards its end. The Act permitted the termination of the licence after 21 years and every seven years thereafter. For company-owned operations this sword of Damocles meant that the threat of municipalisation was ever present and, even if never exercised, was sufficient to ensure that modernisation might never take place. The classic example here is the tramways of Bristol; operated throughout their career by a company but with the constant threat of take-over by Bristol Corporation, the system survived through until 1941 operating open-top and unvestibuled trams that would not have been out of place on the first electric tramways built at the end of the 19th century, whereas other systems were operating state-of-the-art modern trams by World War II.

This volume is one of a series that cover the tramways of England.

Brighton District Tramways

The first street tramway to serve the Brighton area was the Brighton District Tramways. Construction of this line was authorised by the Brighton District Tramways Act of 1882. Although the company sought to gain access through to Brighton itself, the steadfast opposition of the Hove commissioners prevented powers for an eastward extension being granted.

Following construction of the line – which stretched from the boundary between Hove and Aldrington at Westbourne Gardens westwards to a point just south of Shoreham station (a distance of just under 4¾ miles) – passenger services over the 3ft 6in tramway commenced operation on 3 July 1884. The majority of the route was single track with loops and the depot was situated just south of Southwick station.

Initial operation of the new tramway was by steam traction, with three steam engines supplied – two by William Wilkinson & Co Ltd of Pemberton, near Wigan, for the line's opening and one by Aveling & Porter (Invicta Works, Rochester, Kent) two years later (but not used in service until late the following year). Passenger accommodation was provided by two double-deck trailer cars built by the Falcon Engine & Car Works – the future Brush – of Loughborough. In order to provide a link through to Brighton, a horse bus service was operated from Westbourne Gardens to the centre.

The operation of the steam locomotives and trailers was not wholly successful and, following the purchase of three new trams, horse tram operation was introduced on 23 May 1885 to supplement the existing steam trams. These first horse trams were single-deck; later in the year a further seven horse trams, this time double-deck, were acquired.

The company was also weak financially – running almost directly parallel to the London, Brighton & South Coast Railway from Shoreham was not advantageous, particularly as the mainline railway had the competitive edge in being able to serve Brighton direct – and, in 1888, the original company collapsed, with its assets passing to a new company – the Brighton & District Tramway Co Ltd. This new company was not to last long and in May 1889 a liquidator was appointed. A new company – the Brighton & Shoreham Tramways Co Ltd – was set up the same year and recommenced operation in November 1889. The fleet that the company inherited was reduced to only four trams – the three single-deck horse trams plus one of the double-deck

cars – but further trams were acquired in 1891 (five double-deck cars) and 1900 (three single-deck). Eventually, all the double-deck cars were cut down to single-deck. The new owners operated only horse trams, with the result that the three steam engines were disposed of, the two Wilkinson engines being sold to the Wigan & District Tramways Co in 1893.

In 1898 the company was acquired by British Electric Traction Ltd. This company was in the process of acquiring a portfolio of horse and steam tram operations nationwide, with a view to converting them to electric traction and to extending their operations. The new owners had plans for the development of the Brighton & Shoreham and obtained powers for this work. In this, however, they were still thwarted by the opposition of Hove; this culminated in 1911 when Hove Borough Council obtained powers to operate trolleybuses and to remove tram track within its – by now extended – boundaries. The Council swiftly removed the track from the section west from Westbourne Gardens along New Church Road. With its services severely curtailed, horse operation of the remaining section of the Brighton

& Shoreham continued through until all services ceased on 6 June 1913.

Brighton Corporation

Although there had been proposals for the construction of street tramways in Brighton during the last years of the 19th century, these had come to nothing and it was not until 1900 that Brighton Corporation obtained its first powers to construct a new electric tramway. The first Act – which received its royal assent on 30 July 1901 – was followed by further acts in 1902 and 1903 that, amongst other powers, permitted the corporation to construct and operate its own power station. This was constructed at Southwick.

Whilst there was some debate about the choice of gauge for the new tramway, 3ft 6in was eventually settled on and construction started. The first trams – operating over the Lewes Road route – commenced operation on 25 November 1901. By February 1902 all the lines authorised by the 1900 Act were open; these included the loop that ran via Viaduct Road, Beaconsfield Road, Preston Drove and Ditchling Road, the line along Elm Grove to Race Hill, along New England Road to Seven Dials and that south from Elm Grove along Queens Road to Upper Rock Gardens.

The 1902 Act sanctioned the construction of two significant extensions. The first of these to be completed was the section from the west end of Viaduct Road – Preston Circus – south over London Road and York Place to Victoria Gardens; this opened in 1903. The second was the loop south from Victoria Gardens to Old Steine that served the Aquarium terminus; this was to open in July 1904. The 1903 Act authorised the construction of one major extension – that along Dyke Road – plus the line in the centre from Victoria Gardens to the railway station along North Road and Queen's Road; both of these were opened to passenger service on 27 July 1904 and represented the last extensions to the system. Also authorised by the 1903 Act – but never completed – was a second route to the main railway station from Seven Dials via Buckingham Place and Terminus Road. Authorised in 1919 – but again never completed – was a further one-mile extension beyond the Lewes Road terminus to serve Moulsecoomb and a new housing estate. The final extensions took the system to its maximum of just under 9½ route miles. One depot was completed; this was close to the terminus of the Lewes Road route and also served as the corporation's main workshops.

In order to identify the routes, letters – rather than numbers – were introduced in 1902. Following the completion of the system in 1904, routes B and D served the Ditching Road circular, with route B running clockwise and route D running anticlockwise. Route C linked Seven Dials with Race Hill; route E served Race Hill; route L served Lewes Road; route M linked Lewes Road with Seven Dials; route N served Dyke Road; route Q served Rock Gardens – this service involved a reversal at the crossover immediately to the east of the junction between Queen's Park Road and Elm Grove; and route S served the station. Apart from routes C and M, all other routes terminated in the centre at the Aquarium. There was also a tourist tram service – route T – that made the circuitous trip from the Aquarium to Race Hill and returned via Dyke Road and the Ditchling Road circular. This service was introduced on 3 July 1905. Passengers travelled on the top deck only to ensure that they gained the maximum from the spectacular views available.

The later years of the tram service

With the tramway network now at its maximum extent the history of the system over the next two decades or so was marked by improvements to the fleet and by other changes – such as the introduction of passenger shelters.

In 1914 the original fleet of 50 Class A trams was expanded by three new trams; these were the first of the Class B cars to be completed and were the first trams to be built at Lewes Road. Thereafter, all new and replacement trams were constructed by the corporation. During World War I, as a result of the difficulties in obtaining spare parts, a number of the United Electric Car Co-built batch of trams – Nos 41-50 – were converted temporarily to trailer operation. No 12 was also partially rebuilt during the war, whilst No 10 was completely rebuilt following a serious accident.

Both towards the end of the conflict and immediately after the cessation of hostilities, work continued to expand and replace the fleet. Plans were also made for the extension of the Lewes Road route to serve a new housing estate at Moulsecoomb; these were, however, never to be progressed.

In 1929 it was decided that all traffic between St Peter's Church and the Aquarium around Victoria Gardens and Old Steine was to be converted to one-way. All was to operate in a clockwise direction save for a short section of two-way traffic along part of Pavilion Parade. The trams had historically operated anti-clockwise around the loop and so work was undertaken overnight to alter the layout; this was completed and the new arrangements came into operation on 5 May 1929.

Improvements continued to the tram fleet through the 1930s, with the final Class F trams being delivered as late as 1937. By this date, however, there were rumblings that the trams might not have a long-term future. As early as 1930 the corporation and the local bus operators had sought a scheme for the co-ordination of services, but it was not until 1938 that parliament gave sanction for a joint operating agreement between the corporation and the bus operator Brighton, Hove & District. In addition, it was agreed that all tram services were to be converted to trolleybus operation with the exception of that part of the Dyke Road route in Hove.

Following signature of the agreement on 1 April 1939, the process of abandoning the tramway system proceeded rapidly. The Dyke Road route beyond Seven Dials was converted to bus operation on 26 April. On 1 June the Lewes Road route was converted to trolleybus operation, although the track remained operational as far as the depot. On 1 July trams on the circular routes via Beaconsfield and Ditchling were replaced by trolleybuses, and on 17 July the remains of the route to Dyke Road and that to the station were replaced. However, there was to be a short reprieve – between 8 and 10 August – for the section to the station in order to cater for the traffic to and from Brighton races. The final two sections – from Seven Dials to Race Hill and Old Steine to Rock Gardens – closed on 31 August 1939, with the last car – No 41 – arriving back at the depot for the last time from Rock Gardens early on 1 September, just as the Germans launched their *Blitzkrieg* on Poland. Elsewhere, the outbreak of World War II led to tramways being reprieved or recently closed sections reopening, though there was to be no such resurrection for Brighton's system.

The Tramcar Fleet

For the opening of the system in 1901, 30 open-top cars – Nos 1-30 – were supplied by G. F. Milnes & Co; these were fitted with Peckham Pendulum four-wheel trucks, though many were subsequently to receive replacement Brill 21E four-wheel trucks. These were followed in 1902 by a further batch of 10 (Nos 31-40) Milnes-built trams – this time on Brush A four-wheel trucks – and a further 10 – Nos 41-50 – supplied by the United Electric Car Co during 1904 and 1905. This batch of trams was supplied on Brill 21E four-

wheel trucks and it was on this type of truck that all later trams were operated. The original Nos 1-50 were designated Class A. A number of the Nos 41-50 batch were temporarily demotored during World War I and used as trailers, being restored as power cars after the war.

The trams delivered during 1904 and 1905 were the last to be supplied by outside contractors, and the next three trams – Class B Nos 51-53, built in 1914 – were constructed by the corporation at its Lewes Road works, as were all the trams built after World War I. Class B Nos 54-63 were delivered between 1919 and 1922, Class D Nos 64-67 in 1929 and Class E Nos 68-80 between 1929 and 1931. In addition to these trams, the corporation also built replacement trams for older cars in the fleet, with 51 of these completed between 1917 and 1926 – 43 Class B and eight Class C – and a further 35 – four Class E and 31 Class F – between 1932 and 1937. These replacement trams utilised the fleet numbers of withdrawn trams whilst those constructed during the 1930s inherited the trucks from the trams that they replaced. Thus, during the 38-year history of the system, certain fleet numbers were utilised no fewer than three times.

All of the trams were open-top as a result of Board of Trade restrictions on the operation of narrow-gauge trams on systems with significant gradients, but, from the batch of eight replacement trams constructed between 1926 and 1928, all newly-completed bodies were fitted with enclosed lower-deck vestibules.

Although no Brighton tram was preserved when the system closed, one of the later replacement trams – No 53 of 1937 – was eventually rescued after many years on a pig farm and then undercover storage. Now owned by the Brighton 53 Group, the tram is currently under restoration.

Volk's Electric Railway

Magnus Volk (1851-1937) was a noted local inventor and entrepreneur. Keen to exploit the potential of electricity to operate a tramway, he sought – and obtained – permission to open a short line, built along the seafront in Brighton. The 2ft 0in-gauge line, which extended a distance of about 400m, opened on 4 August 1883. The line was an immediate success but was damaged by the sea the following month. Volk, however, was

ambitious and, again with permission, he rebuilt and extended the line – this time to the gauge (which is still used) of 2ft 8½in – to Paston Place. The new line opened on 4 April 1884 and was now some 1,300m in length, but was to be further extended to Black Rock following the demise of the Brighton & Rottingdean. With this new extension opening in May 1901, the line now ran for a distance of some 2km.

In 1930 the line was shortened by some 180m at its western end but, in its place, a new – and grander – Aquarium terminus was opened on 27 June 1930. At the eastern end, the construction of a new lido at Black Rock in 1937 resulted in a further reduction of some 180m in the length of the line. Throughout this period the railway was privately owned but, on 1 April 1940, ownership passed to Brighton Corporation; the council still owns the line today. Services were suspended during World War II and on resumption in 1948 much remedial work had been undertaken to repair damage and some additional rolling stock acquired – from Southend – to replace stock that was not repaired after the war.

Although threatened with potential closure as a result of deteriorating finances and physical condition during the last two decades of the 20th century, the line has survived and has recently undergone a major renovation project. Proudly boasting to be the world's oldest-surviving electric railway, the restoration project has ensured that Volk's Electric Railway will continue to ply its trade for many years to come.

Brighton & Rottingdean

Volk was keen to see his electric railway extended further east, however, the topography was not ideal and he sought a radical alternative solution; this was the extraordinary Brighton & Rottingdean Seashore Electric Railway.

Construction commenced in 1894 and, to avoid the cost of a viaduct at Paston Place, Volk decided to lay some of the line along the seabed some 100m from the shore. This resulted in two sets of parallel rails laid on concrete sleepers being embedded in the seabed, with the one vehicle forming a raised platform above the sea.

The line – which was almost 5km in length – opened on 28 November 1896 but was to be severely damaged in a storm less than a week later. With the line and vehicle restored, the line reopened on 20 July 1897. It operated successfully through until 1900, when it was found that erosion – caused by recently erected groynes – had undermined the track. This, combined with the corporation's plans to improve sea defences, required work to be undertaken that Volk could not afford and as a result the line closed in January 1901 and was dismantled.

Volk took the opportunity of extending his other line – the Electric Railway – further to the east. This was achieved by constructing a viaduct immediately to the east of Paston Place; this was to survive – albeit buried in shingle in later years – until it was replaced by a concrete raft in 1991.

A note on the photographs

The majority of the illustrations in this book have been drawn from the collection of the Online Transport Archive, a UK-registered charity that was set up to accommodate collections put together by transport enthusiasts who wished to see their precious images secured for the long-term. Further information about the archive can be found at: www.onlinetransportarchive.org or email secretary@onlinetransportarchive.org.

The proximity of the western terminus of the Brighton & Shoreham Tramways Co Ltd's to the railway station in Shoreham is all too evident in this view. Competition from the London, Brighton & South Coast Railway, which had direct access to the centre of Brighton (unlike the tramway), gave the railway a considerable competitive edge, particularly once Hove Borough Council exercised its powers and removed the track from the section along New Church Road.

Following the takeover of the failed Brighton & District Tramway Co in 1889, the Brighton & Shoreham acquired only four passenger cars. These were supplemented by the purchase of five double-deck trams – Nos 5-9 – in 1891. One of this quintet is shown here; the tram's livery was predominantly yellow. All of the double-deck trams were eventually converted to single deck.

Following the loss of the section along New Church Road in 1911 the surviving section of the Brighton & Shoreham soldiered on until 6 June 1913, when the last services were operated. Here No 10 – one of three single-deck trams acquired by the company in 1900 (the last trams bought) – is seen bedecked with the black wreath that it carried for the final service.

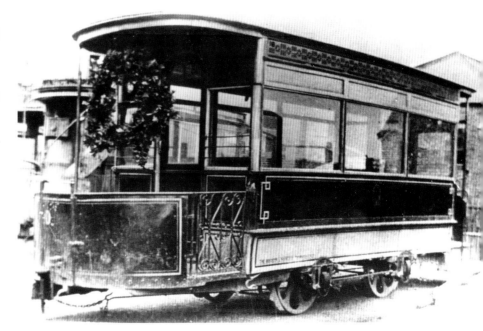

Brighton Corporation possessed a single tram depot situated at Lewes Road, which became operational with the system in November 1901. Following the withdrawal of the trams in 1939, the depot continued in use as a bus and trolleybus depot. It remains a bus depot – albeit with the depot accommodation having been rebuilt – at the present time, now being occupied by Brighton & Hove. Pictured in front of the depot is No 32; this was one of the replacement trams and entered service in 1925, and one of the 21 Class B trams still in service when the system closed. Note the route letter in the centre of the upper panel rather than above the vestibule; this unusual arrangement was the consequence of the terminal arrangements at the Aquarium. Most intending passengers would approach the trams from the south and thus see the sides first.

Reproduced from a postcard franked 5 August 1911, three Class A trams – with No 30 closest to the camera – stand at the Aquarium terminus. The trams could accommodate 52 seated passengers – 26 on each deck – and this was the same on most of the trams operated by the corporation. The Steine Gardens are still extant – one of the few common features more than a century on – although they've lost their iron railings and are now grassed over rather than being more formal. The majority of the buildings visible in the background are also as much a part of history as the trams.

Pictured awaiting its next duty on a service towards Elm Grove at Old Steine is No 1. This Class E car was the third to bear this fleet number and one of a quartet of replacement trams constructed at Lewes Road during 1932. In the background behind the tram can be seen the top of the Royal York Buildings. This structure, which has its origins in the early 19th century, was originally a hotel but was subsequently converted into offices when acquired by the Council. This building – now listed Grade II – is still extant and has recently been reconverted back into a hotel.

In 1937 the country marked the coronation of King George VI and No 23 stands in front of a celebratory display. At this time No 23 was almost brand-new, one of six Class F trams built at Lewes Road in 1936. The later trams of this type had slightly raised upper-deck decency panels and had lost the brackets on the sides that had been used for the route letters. The livery was modified as well, with red replacing cream on the rocker – i.e. lower – side panels. The original livery is shown to good effect on No 1, seen in the previous photograph.

Class E No 73 – which was new in 1930 – is pictured at Old Steine with a service towards Rock Gardens via Queens Park Road. Trolleybus No 5 is seen on route 26A, a replacement for the tram route D, which had been converted on 1 July 1939. Route Q to Rock Gardens was destined to be one of the last two tram services in Brighton, being converted to trolleybus operation on 31 August 1939.

Another Class E car, No 68, awaits departure from Old Steine with a service towards Queens Park Road. Alongside is trolleybus No 36 on the short-lived service No 40, which replaced tram routes S (to the station) and N, which was the inner section of the Dyke Road route, on 17 July 1939.

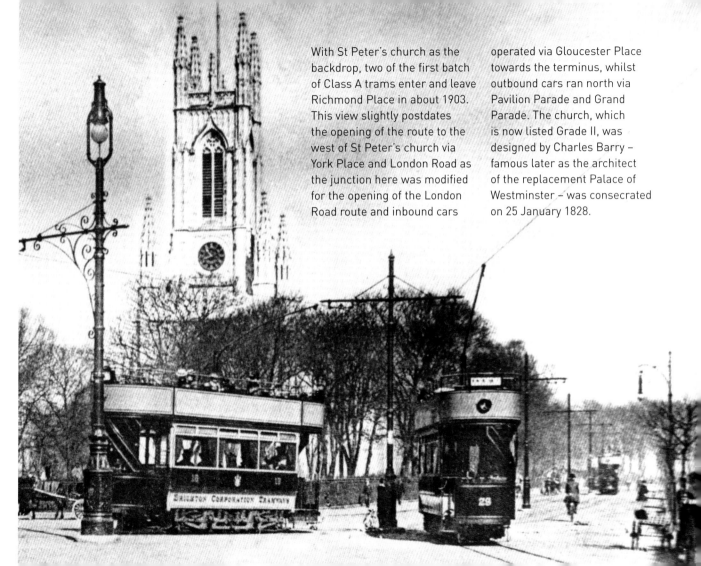

With St Peter's church as the backdrop, two of the first batch of Class A trams enter and leave Richmond Place in about 1903. This view slightly postdates the opening of the route to the west of St Peter's church via York Place and London Road as the junction here was modified for the opening of the London Road route and inbound cars operated via Gloucester Place towards the terminus, whilst outbound cars ran north via Pavilion Parade and Grand Parade. The church, which is now listed Grade II, was designed by Charles Barry – famous later as the architect of the replacement Palace of Westminster – was consecrated on 25 January 1828.

North Gate, Royal Pavilion

PAVILION TERMINUS

For the first two years of the tramway's existence, the main terminus in the centre was located on Marlborough Place, outside the northern gate to the Pavilion. This view looking towards the west along Church Street sees two Class A trams – with No 26 closest to the camera on a service to Ditchling – awaiting departure from the terminus. The view at the eastern end of Church Street is largely recognisable, although a modern traffic island now sits at the junction. The Pavilion dated originally to the late 18th century, but the building that exists today is very much the product of rebuilding work undertaken to the designs of John Nash after 1815. Now Grade I listed and owned by the Council, the Pavilion has undergone considerable restoration over the years to return it to its previous condition whilst in royal ownership.

RAILWAY STATION

Class A No 9 is seen on the stub terminus at Central station – this section of the network had opened on 27 July 1904. The tram displays the original black on white destination blind, which were gradually replaced from 1906 onwards by more legible white on black blinds produced at Lewes Road. The tram is in original condition with reversed stairs, and was to survive in service until 1920.

A further view taken at Central station – but this time after the Grouping of 1923 (note the 'Southern Railway' name on the station façade below the clock) – sees Class B car No 2 awaiting departure for the short downhill trip to the Aquarium. This was a replacement car which entered service in 1923; it was to be scrapped in 1935.

LONDON ROAD

Pictured on a postcard franked 13 February 1905 – less than two years after the opening of the section – is the last of the original batch of Class A trams – No 30 – descending London Road with an inbound service. This tram would survive in service until 1921.

DYKE ROAD

Class F No 58 – one of the type completed at Lewes Road in 1933 – stands at the terminus of the Dyke Road route. The northern section of the Dyke Road route – beyond Seven Dials – was the first tram route in Brighton to be closed and was replaced by buses on 26 April 1939. Although Hove had played host to one of the early trolleybus experiments in Britain before World War I, it had vehemently opposed the introduction of overhead into the area and, as this section of route was controlled by Hove, the trams were replaced by buses rather than trolleybuses. Note the lamp above the tram; this was used to provide illumination at night to assist the conductor in swinging the trolleypole round.

Pictured at the Dyke Road terminus towards the end of the system's life is No 74; this was a Class F car that was new in 1936 and replaced Class E No 74, which had been scrapped earlier in the year following an accident. In the background can be seen one of the wooden-built tram shelters that were a feature of a number of Brighton tram termini, with other examples at Race Hill and Ditchling Road.

DITCHLING ROAD

Two Class F trams pass at the top of Ditchling Road on the Beaconsfield-Ditchling circular route heading into and out of Preston Drove; on the left, No 48 is on route D and, on the right, No 42 is on route B. No 42 was new in 1934 whilst No 48 was completed the following year. Although the shops in the background are still extant, the attractive tram shelter – like the trams themselves – is long gone.

During July 1938, Class F No 51 descends Ditchling Road with an inbound service; the tram was one of three built the previous year. The trio were destined to have barely two years' operation before the system closed at the end of August 1939.

On the tram: ANZORA HAIR CREAM — "WON'T SOIL LINEN" — LEWES Rᴰ — 26 — 26 — BRIGHTON CORPORATION TRAMWAYS

LEWES ROAD

The first of the Class E cars were four replacements – Nos 1, 7, 17 and 26 – that were constructed at Lewes Road works in 1932. This view records No 26, when new, standing on Lewes Road at its junction with Union Road. All of the Class E cars survived until the system's closure with the exception of No 74, which was scrapped and replaced following an accident in 1936.

In 1914 the existing fleet was increased by the construction of three new trams – Nos 51-53 – at Lewes Road. These were the first of the Class B cars, of which 56 were built between then and 1926, and one of the trio – No 52 – is seen here at the terminus of route L on Lewes Road. The terminus was a short distance north of the depot; when the service was converted to trolleybus operation, the track as far as the depot remained open for depot workings only. The crew pictured are in the process of 'changing ends'; the driver is removing the key from the controller prior to walking to the other end of the tram. There were plans – never progressed – for the extension of the line north to Moulsecoomb.

No 52 was one of two trams – the other being No 51 – that were delivered with 54 seats rather than the usual 52 – with 28 on the upper deck – for use as tourist cars during the summer. No 52 was withdrawn in 1937, being replaced by a new Class F car of the same number.

Pictured making use of the trolley reverser at Elm Grove is the replacement No 52, which was completed at Lewes Road in 1937. With the signature on the co-ordination agreement on 1 April 1939 and the decision to convert the tram system to bus and trolleybus operation, No 52 was destined to have an operational life of only two years.

ROCK GARDENS

The southern terminus of the Queen's Park route was situated at the junction of Upper Rock Gardens and St James's Street. Here Class A No 4 – in original condition with Peckham Cantilever truck and reversed stairs – stands at the Rock Gardens terminus. The wood used in the bodies of this first batch of trams – Nos 1-30 – was found to be unsatisfactory and all had subsequently to be rebuilt. No 4 was destined to survive in service until 1924.

THE END

Such was the precipitate nature of the tramway abandonment in Brighton that, in order to cater for the crowds travelling to and from the racecourse for the meeting of 8 to 10 August 1939, the route to the station was reopened and some 40 trams reinstated. This is a view from the Race Hill terminus – with Class E No 73 closest to the camera – taken during the final swan song of the Brighton system. Less than a month later the trams were no more and Britain was at war.

Following their withdrawal, the majority of Brighton's tram fleet was broken up in front of the depot on Lewes Road. Awaiting their fate in this view are Class E car No 17, which was new in 1932, and Class F No 59, which entered service the following year. Notice the crude sign offering seats and cushions for sale, the latter available for 2s 6d each.

Following the abandonment, the then general manager had the body of the works car transferred to his garden for use as a shed. He also recorded many aspects of the final days of the tramway system and the introduction of trolleybuses on ciné film.

THE TRAM FLEET

Between 1901 and 1905 the corporation took delivery of 50 open-top four-wheel cars that were to be designated Class A. Nos 1-30 were supplied by G. F. Milnes & Co in 1901 and originally fitted with Peckham Pendulum trucks, but these were replaced by Brill 21E trucks between 1908 and 1913. The following year Milnes supplied a further 10 – Nos 31-40 – that were fitted with Brush A trucks. The final 10 – Nos 41-50 – were built by the United Electric Car Co Ltd during 1904 and 1905; these were fitted with the more reliable Brill 21E truck from new and this type of truck was to be used for the remainder of the fleet. No 11 shows to good effect the reversed stairs used on these trams as well as the wire mesh lifeguard. The reversed stairs caused problems for the driver's vision as they obscured the view of the near side. The Class A trams were also fitted with double doors between the platforms and the lower saloon.

Between 1914 and 1926 the corporation constructed 57 Class B trams at Lewes Road. These were all fitted with Brill 21E four-wheel trucks and had normal staircases rather than reversed. No 19 is pictured here in Lewes Road depot.

Class C No 34 – the second tram to carry this fleet number – has just arrived at Central station. This view can be dated towards the end of the system's life as the station proclaims the arrival of 'Southern Electric' services; electric services on the ex-London, Brighton & South Coast Railway main line to Brighton commenced operation on 1 January 1933. No 34 was one of eight trams – the others being Nos 10, 13, 22, 35, 37, 40 and 45 (all the second to carry the fleet number, with the exception of No 10, which was the third) – constructed at Lewes Road during 1926 and 1927. These were the first trams in the fleet to be fitted with enclosed lower-deck vestibules; in order to accommodate the space required to turn the handbrake, all were also fitted with slightly lengthened platforms. All were to survive until the final closure of the system in 1939.

There were only four members of Class D – Nos 64-67 – and No 66 is pictured here shortly after the system closed, awaiting its fate. All were built at Lewes Road on Brill 21E trucks with bodies completed in gurjan or pyinkado rather than teak. The bodies also had convex lower-deck rocker panels, rather than concave. All survived until the system's closure.

Between 1929 and 1931 13 Class E cars were built at Lewes Road; Nos 68-80 were followed in 1932 by four additional replacement cars. These were No 1, 7, 17 and 26, which were all the third trams to bear these fleet numbers. No 68 is seen here at the Aquarium terminus alongside Class C No 13 in August 1936.

Between 1933 and 1937 the corporation constructed 31 replacement cars at Lewes Road, designated Class F and similar to No 26, seen here. These were Nos 2, 9, 11, 14, 15, 20, 21, 23-25, 27, 30, 41-43, 46 and 48-50, which were the third cars to bear these fleet numbers, and Nos 51-60, 63 and 74, which were the second. One of the type, No 53, is currently undergoing restoration – the only Brighton Corporation electric tramcar to survive.

This is the lower-deck interior of No 23 – a Class F car that was new in 1935 – seen in 1936.

Right: Aside from its passenger fleet, Brighton Corporation also possessed one dedicated works car – No 1 – which was delivered in 1910 as a snowplough. The origins of the vehicle are uncertain but it was modified during its career to also act as a railgrinder and general works car.

Brighton 53

THE FRENCH VISITORS AT BRIGHTON
VOLK'S RAILWAY TOUR.

VOLK'S ELECTRIC RAILWAY

Following the opening of the Palace Pier in 1901 the station serving Volk's Electric Railway was rebuilt. It is pictured here in 1904 on the occasion of an official visit to Brighton by a French delegation in connection with the recent signing of the Entente Cordiale. The short section from the Palace Pier to the new terminus at Aquarium was closed to permit road widening and the new Aquarium terminus opened on 27 June 1930.

Viewed from the Banjo Pier, one of the Volk's Electric Railway cars makes its way along the viaduct, to the east of Paston Place, through a very stormy sea. The viaduct was constructed following the closure of the Brighton & Rottingdean Electric Railway to permit the extension of the Volk's line to Black Rock. Over the years shingle built up around the viaduct and buried it, although, as a structure, it was to survive until rebuilding in the early 1990s.

On 22 May 1948 Volk's Electric Railway No 1 is pictured departing from the Aquarium terminus. This car had originally been numbered 10 when new in 1926 and had only just been renumbered 1 when recorded in this view. It reverted to its original fleet number in 2000 and was recently restored by Alan Keef Ltd as part of the major refurbishment of the line completed in 2018.

Approaching the section of line that passed through the depot and workshop at Paston Place on 4 May 1952 is No 2. The car has just passed over the Banjo Pier and beyond can be seen the track on the now buried viaduct. No 2 was built in 1910 as No 9 and was to be renumbered in 1948 following the acquisition of the two cars from the Southend Pier Railway. It reverted to its original number in 2000 and remains in service on the refurbished line. The depot and workshop complex, from which this photograph was taken, was demolished in 2016, having been deemed unsafe, and was completely rebuilt as part of the refurbishment project.

Pictured at the old terminus of Aquarium, which was also subject to rebuilding as part of the recent refurbishment project, is No 6, originally built in 1901. This was one of three cars completed that year in connection with the extension eastwards to Black Rock. These were originally designed to carry 32 passengers but all were extended to increase their seating capacity to 40. Out of use for some time, No 6 was one of the cars restored by Alan Keef Ltd as part of the recent project.

During the 1930s the construction of the new lido at Black Rock resulted in Volk's Electric Railway being slightly cut back. Pictured at the new terminus in the mid-1950s is No 2. This station was to last until 1998, when a new station was completed in connection with work to create a storm water storage scheme for the new marina.

VOLK'S ELECTRIC RAILWAY
BLACK ROCK STATION

The only vehicle operated by the Brighton & Rottingdean was supplied by the Gloucester Railway Carriage & Wagon Co; known officially as *Pioneer* and unofficially as 'Daddy Long-legs', the vehicle was designated as seagoing and, as a result, had to be equipped with lifebelts and a lifeboat. The driver also had to be a qualified captain of a sea-going vessel. The line was promoted as 'A sea voyage on wheels'. The tram is seen here fully-loaded with passengers at Paston Place. The low tide allows for a good view of the way that the vehicle was raised above the sea by iron supports; these were supported on wheels that ran along two sets of parallel tracks – each 825mm apart – with a total gauge from outer rail to outer rail of 5.5m. Power for the vehicle was obtained by a trolleypole that ran under catenary strung above the line.

STEEP GRADE RAILWAY

Now owned by the National Trust, the Devil's Dyke is a 100m deep valley that was a very popular local attraction in the late 19th and early 20th centuries; for example, 30,000 visited on Whit Monday in 1893. A number of transport plans were developed to take the crowds to and from the site, including a railway branch built by the London, Brighton & South Coast Railway that operated from 1887 until 1939. Another was the Steep Grade Railway, which opened on 24 July 1897 and provided two independent cable-operated parallel lines – each of 3ft 0in gauge – to convey passengers a distance of some 256m. The line was not, however, a financial success and closed completely early in the following decade.

CREDITS

Lost Tramways of England – Brighton
Published in Great Britain in 2019
by Graffeg Limited

Written by Peter Waller copyright © 2019.
Designed and produced by Graffeg Limited
copyright © 2019.

Graffeg Limited, 24 Stradey Park Business
Centre, Mwrwg Road, Llangennech, Llanelli,
Carmarthenshire SA14 8YP Wales UK
Tel 01554 824000 www.graffeg.com

Peter Waller is hereby identified as the
author of this work in accordance with
section 77 of the Copyrights, Designs and
Patents Act 1988.

A CIP Catalogue record for this book is
available from the British Library.

ISBN 9781912654376

1 2 3 4 5 6 7 8 9

Photo credits

© Barry Cross Collection/Online Transport
Archive: pages 12, 14, 15, 18, 20, 22, 27, 31,
42, 45, 46, 54, 62.
© W. A. Camwell/National Tramway
Museum: pages 16, 33, 35, 48, 51.
© D. W. K. Jones Collection/Online Transport
Archive: pages 17, 24, 25, 29, 30, 40, 52, 53, 63.
© F. K. Farrell Collection/Online Transport
Archive: pages 34, 36, 37, 41, 49, 50, 57.
© Hugh Nicol/National Tramway Museum:
page 39.
© C. Carter/Online Transport Archive:
page 47.
© John Meredith/Online Transport Archive:
pages 58, 59.
© F. E. J. Ward/Online Transport Archive:
page 60.
© Phil Tatt/Online Transport Archive: page 61.

The photographs used in this book have
come from a variety of sources. Wherever
possible contributors have been identified
although some images may have been used
without credit or acknowledgement and if
this is the case apologies are offered and
full credit will be given in any future edition.

Cover: Railway station.

Back cover: Pavilion Terminus, Double-deck
Tram, Tram at Lewes Road.

Lost Tramways of Wales series:

- **Cardiff** ISBN 9781912213122
- **North Wales** ISBN 9781912213139
- **South Wales and Valleys**
  ISBN 9781912213146
- **Swansea and Mumbles**
  ISBN 9781912213153

Lost Tramways of England series:

- **Bristol** ISBN 9781912654345
- **Coventry** ISBN 9781912654338
- **Nottingham** ISBN 9781912654352
- **Southampton** ISBN 9781912654369
- **Brighton** ISBN 9781912654376
- **Bradford** ISBN 9781912654406
- **Birmingham North** ISBN 9781912654390
- **Birmingham South** ISBN 9781912654383

Lost Tramways of Scotland series:

- **Aberdeen** ISBN 9781912654413
- **Dundee** ISBN 9781912654420